Jamaican Sayings

Character

Other titles in the series:

Jamaican Sayings
Life

Jamaican Sayings
Success

Andrea Campbell

I am grateful to my family

– Richmond and Shari –

for their love and support without which this book would not have been possible.

Jamaican Sayings

Character

Andrea M. Campbell

MBA MA

Publisher: AA Global Sourcing Ltd

Website: http://www.aaglobalsourcing.com

First Edition

First published in Great Britain in 2012 by

AA Global Sourcing Ltd

http://www.aaglobalsourcing.com

A catalogue record for this book is available from The British Library

ISBN: 978-1-4716-8887-4

Table of Contents

On the cover:

Green Anole
Saltwater Crocodile
The Doctor Bird (Trochilus polytmus)
- the national bird
Woodpecker
Jamaican Coney

Introduction

Jamaican Sayings - Character is the second in a series of three books that capture Jamaican adages used to communicate ideas about human nature, behaviour, relationships, aspirations, health hope and survival. *Jamaican Sayings - Life* and *Jamaican Sayings - Success* complement the series.

The adages represent an archive of the wit and wisdom of many generations and aim to trigger reflection and thought. In their use they are never fully explained but those to whom they are directed usually understand their meaning based on the context in which they are used. They utilise imagery and draw upon a variety of flora and fauna to enrich their content. They hold valuable lessons, inspiration and wisdom that link Jamaican culture to its African past.

The sayings are presented in three parts:

i) the original saying;
ii) the literal English translation and
iii) the meaning it aims to convey.

As outlined in the contents, Jamaican Sayings – Character contains information on Jamaica's food and drink, tea, flora, fauna, flowers, official visits and parishes.

1. Ah fass mek Anancy deh ah house tap

It's because Anancy is inquisitive why he is living in the ceiling

Mind your own business or you could find yourself in trouble or isolated.

2. Ah greedy mek fly fallaw coffin go ah hole

It's because of greed why a fly follows a coffin to the grave

Greed is the root of all evil; it can bring your downfall.

3. Ah noh ebery chain yuh ear ah rolling calf

It's not every chain that you hear that is a rolling calf

Bad news is often exaggerated; don't always assume the worst.

4. Ah noh ebery rainfall mus wet yuh

It is not every rainfall that should wet you

You don't have to be a part of everything; let some things go by.

5. Ah noh everyting good fi eat good fi talk

It is not everything that is good to eat is also good to discuss

Some things are better left unspoken; don't repeat everything you hear!

6. Alligetta shouden call hog lang mout

An alligator should not refer to a hog as 'long mouth'

Be careful not to ridicule or belittle someone who has similar characteristics to you.

7. A tayla nebber av a good suit

A tailor never owns a good suit

People should practise what they preach and lead by example.

8. Ax me no question ah tell yuh no lie

Ask me no question, I will tell youno lie

Avoid excessive questioning, lest you receive false information.

9. Behine dawg ah dawg, in front ah dawg ah Missa Dawg

Behind dog is Dog"; in front of dog is "Mr. Dog"

People disrespect you in your absence but not generally in your presence.

10. Bline man see im neighba fault

A blind man sees his neighbour's faults

Too often we are blind to our own shortcomings but quick to point out those of others.

11. Black fowl noh fi yuh, yuh call im jankro

If a black fowl is not yours, you will call him vulture

People tend to think that what they have is better than those of others even when it is clear that they are exactly the same.

12. Bowl go, buggy come

A bowl goes a buggy comes

If you give even a little you will receive a lot in return; be kind!

13. Bucket wid hole ah battam noh bizniz ah rivaside

A bucket with a hole in the bottom has no business at the riverside

Keep out of people's business, especially when you have secrets yourself.

14. Bush hab aise, wall hab yeye

Bush has ears and wall has eyes

Be careful what you say as news travels fast (and sometimes mysteriously).

15. Cack mout kill cack

A cock's mouth will kill him

If you talk too much, your own words will condemn you.

16. Cackroach nebber so drunk dat im walk inna fowl yard

Cockroach is never so drunk that he walks into a fowl's yard

i) If you value your life you will keep away from those who threaten to destroy it;
ii) Never put yourself into unnecessary danger.

17. Cackroach noh business inna fowl fight

A cockroach has no business in a fowl fight

Keep out of other people's business.

18. Cap noh fit yuh noh tek ih up

If a cap doesn't fit you leave it alone

Keep out of issues that don't concern you.

19. Chink nebber run till im si crowd

A bedbug doesn't reveal itself until it sees a crowd

i) Your vulnerabilities are often exposed when you least expect it;
ii) Some people tend to behave badly when they have an audience.

20. Cow noh hab noh business inna hawse-play

Cows have no business in horse-play

People should mind their own business.

21. Cow dat belong ah butcha nebber seh im berry well

A cow that belongs to a butcher never says that it is very well

Sometimes you have to lie to save yourself.

22. Crab know seh im back noh strong im noh dig ole

Crab says that he knows his back isn't strong so he doesn't dig a hole

Don't get into situations where you know that you will not be able to handle or bear the consequences.

23. Craben choke puppy

Craven chokes puppy

If you are greedy you will get hurt.

24. Cuss dawg but nebber seh im teeth noh white

You can curse a dog, but never say that its teeth aren't white

Give credit where it is due; don't allow people's faults to rob you of your objectivity.

25. Dawg-flea tell im pickney im mustn't seh im dead till im ketch pan finger nail

Dog flea told his child that he shouldn't say that he is dead until he is caught in someone's finger nail

Don't write people off as long as they're alive. (While there's life there's hope)

26. Dawg lib well im trouble cow ah pass

A dog that has a good life bothers cows

Those who can afford not to work will spend their time interfering with others.

27. De bes ah field mus hab weed

Even the best fields have weeds

No-one is perfect.

28. Def eaz gi liad chouble

Deaf ears cause trouble for liars

i) If you don't listen or if you cannot hear what is being said, you risk misinterpreting it;
ii) Avoid passing on incorrect information.

29. Di hiya di monkey clime, di more im expose

The higher the monkey climbs the more it is exposed

The higher people climb up the social ladder the more their character is revealed.

30. Di wises man ah sometimes fool

The wisest man is sometimes a fool

Everyone has moments of vulnerability.

31. Dish claat com tun table towel

A dish-cloth becomes a table towel

Some people who are not accustomed to having expensive things tend to show off when their fortune changes.

32. Draft steer nebber mek saddle hawse

A draft steer never turns into a saddle horse

Some people are far too crude and rough to ever becoming refined.

33. Drunk man talk di truth

A drunken man speaks the truth

When people are under the influence of alcohol they invariably speak the truth.

34. Dry stump ah cane piece noh fi laugh when cane piece ketch ah fire

A dry stump in a cane plantation should not laugh when the plantation ignites

Don't rejoice at other people's demise; you could be more vulnerable than you think!

35. Eat wid di deble but gi'im a long spoon

Eat with the devil but give him a long spoon

You have to associate with all kinds of people but they don't have to become your friends.

36. Ebery cave-hole hab im own duppy

Every cave has its own ghost

Everyone has secrets and everyone faces challenges.

37. Ebery dawg tink im ah lian inna im massa yard

Every dog thinks he is a lion in his master's yard

People are more confident and powerful when they are on their own territory.

38. Every day bucket ah go ah well, one day di battom ah go drap out

Every day the bucket is taken to the well, one day the bottom will drop out

Those who consistently take risks will get caught eventually.

39. Ebery day deble help tief one day God wi elp watchman

Every day the devil helps the thief, one day God will help the watchman

People who consistently do wrong will eventually be caught.

40. Ebery pot haffi siddung pan im own batty

Every pot has to sit down on its own bottom

Every man must be responsible for himself; be independent!

41. Empty barrel mek di mose naize

Empty barrel makes the most noise

People conceal their ignorance by pretending to be very knowledgeable about a subject.

42. Falla fashan mek monkey lose im tail

A monkey that follows fashion will lose its tail

Don't get into the habit of copying other people's habits; be original!

43. Finger nebber seh "look yah," ih seh "look deh"

A finger never says "look here"; it says "look there"

People don't usually focus on their own faults; they seek instead to find the faults of others.

44. Finger tink yuh cyaan cut ih off an trow ih weh

Even if your finger stinks you cannot cut it off and throw it away

Support your friends and family if they are in trouble, irrespective of the mistakes that they may have made.

45. Fowl nyam done im rub im mout pan grung

A fowl finishes eating then it rubs its mouth on the ground

Some people are particularly ungrateful.

46. Fowl seh im noh business inna mongoose politics

A fowl says that he has no business in mongoose politics

Mind your own business.

47. Fox cyaan ketch di grape im seh ih sour

The fox cannot reach the grape he says it's sour

People will speak ill of you if they are unable to get what they want from you.

48. Frog nebber gargle im troat till im tase fresh wahta

A frog never gargle its throat until it tastes fresh water

Some people just love to show off when strangers are around.

49. Frog seh wat is joke to yuh is det to mi

Frog says that what is joke to you is death to him

Don't amuse yourself at another person's expense.

50. Gi yuh hawse yuh waan saggle

I gave you a horse, now you want a saddle too

Some people will never be satisfied with what they are given; they always want more.

51. God Almighty know why im bruk fowl wing

God knows why he broke fowl wings

Some people are simply too arrogant and have to be humbled.

52. God mek man strait, ah rum mek im fall dung

God made man upright but rum makes him fall to the ground

An individual who is under the influence of alcohol is prone to doing silly things.

53. Haard aise mek a soft behind

"Hard ears" make a soft bottom

Disobedient children will be duly punished.

54. Haard aise pickney nyam rackstone

"Hard ears" children eat rock stone

Children who disobey their parents will have a hard life.

55. Haard aise pickney walk two time

"Hard ears" children walk twice

Those who insist on being stubborn will suffer unduly.

56. Haard ah hearing pickney ded ah sun hot

A disobedient child dies from the heat of the sun

Children who will not heed advice will struggle in life.

57. Han go paki come

A hand goes out,a calabash comes in

If you are in the habit of helping others you in turn will receive support.

58. Hog run fi im life dawg run fi im character

A pig runs for its life, a dog runs for its character

People don't all have the same values; what's important to you may not be important to someone else.

59. Hawse noh too good fi carry im own grass

A horse is never too good to carry its own grass

No one is too good to perform acts that may be regarded as lowly, if it is ultimately to his/her benefit.

60. Howdy an tenk yuh noh bruk noh square

"Hello" and "thank you" do not break any squares

Greeting and thanking people do not require a lot of effort.
(Manners take you throughout the world)

61. Hungry dawg nyam roas kaarn

A hungry dog will eat roast corn

Desperate situations demand desperate measures.

62. Idle man head ah deble workshop

The head of an idle person is a workshop for the devil

The devil finds work for idle hands.

63. Idle man tempt di deble

An idle man tempts the devil

People with nothing to do ultimately get into trouble.

64. If bees nebber hab sting im woulden keep im honey

If bees did not have sting, they wouldn't be able to keep their honey

People have a right to protect their property, even if they are perceived as being mean.

65. If danki bray afta yuh noh bray afta im

If a donkey brays at you, you shouldn't attempt to bray at the donkey

It takes two to quarrel; avoid confrontations by keeping your mouth shut.

66. If fish coulda keep im mouth shut im woulda nebber get caught

If fish had kept its mouth shut it would never have gotten caught

Mind your own business and keep out of trouble.

67. Ih haad fi keep out di debil but ih wos fi drive im out

It is difficult to keep out the devil but even more difficult to drive him out

It is hard to keep out of trouble but harder still to get out once you are involved.

68. If wind noh blow fowl batty noh show

If the wind doesn't blow fowl bottoms aren't exposed

It's only in a crisis that you can see people's true character.

69. If yuh back monkey im wi fight tiga

If you support a monkey it will fight a tiger

Support and encouragement boost people's confidence and they will embrace bigger and more rewarding challenges.

70. If yuh fly wid jankro yuh nyam rotten meat

If you fly with vultures you will eat rotten meat

If you associate with obnoxious people you will soon become like them. (Show me your friends and I'll tell you who you are)

71. If yuh call tiga massa ih wi nyam yuh

If you call the tiger a master, it will devour you

If you are too humble people will trample you.

72. If yuh fallaw wah rivva carry yuh nebber drink di wahta

If you were aware of all that lies in the river you would never drink the water

If you were aware of the true character of some people you would avoid them at all costs.

73. If yuh go ah tump-a-foot dance yuh mus dance tump-a-foot

If you go to "tump-a-foot" dance you must dance "tump-a-foot"

When in Rome do as the Romans.

74. If yuh hea di deble ah come clear di way

If you hear the devil coming, clear the way

Keep out of trouble's way.
Some people bring trouble wherever they go; try to avoid them.

75. If yuh lib wid dawg yuh larn fi bark

If you live with dogs you'll learn to bark

You are influenced by those with whom you associate.
(Show me your friends and I'll tell you who you are)

76. If yuh lie wid dawg yuh wi rise wid fleas

If you lie with a dog you are certain to rise with fleas

It is easy to assume the bad habits of those with whom we keep company.

77. If yuh lie yuh wi tief

If you lie you will steal

Lying and stealing go together; never trust a liar!

78. If yuh lob licky-licky pot wi bun yuh finga

If you love pickings your fingers will get burnt

Be cautious of gifts and bribes; they could land you in trouble.

79. If yuh noh go unda fowl roost fowl cyaan shit pon yuh

If you don't go under fowl roosts, fowls won't be able to defecate on you

Keep away from trouble and you won't be blamed for anything that happens.

80. If yuh noh hab good fi seh noh seh nuttn

If you have nothing good to say don't say anything

It's better not to say anything than to speak negatively about people.

81. If yuh noh waah leaf drop pan yuh tan fram unda di tree

If you don't want leaf to drop on you don't go under the tree

Avoid situations that can have undesirable consequence or in which you can be blamed.

82. If yuh play wid fire yuh wi get bun

If you play with fire you will get burnt

If you continuously involve yourself in dangerous situations you will eventually get hurt.

83. If yuh spit in di sky ih will fall in yuh eye

If you spit in the sky it will fall in your eye

If you ill-treat people, in due course you in turn will be ill-treated; show gratitude!

84. If yuh throw stoane in a hog pen di one weh bawl out ah im get di lick

If you throw stone in a pigsty, the one that cries out is the one that was hit

People are who they reveal themselves to be, not who we think they are.

85. If yuh waah fi ride far spare di hawse

If you want to ride far, spare the horse

Treat people with respect and they will go the extra mile for you.

86. If yuh doan mash ants yuh doan fine im gut

If you don't mash an ant, you won't find its gut

People's true personality emerges when you have a dispute with them.

87. If yuh waah fi know yuh fren lay down ah roadside farm drunk

If you want to know who your friends are, lay down by the roadside and pretend to be drunk

Your true friends acknowledge you not only in the good times but also in the difficult times. (A friend in need is a friend indeed)

88. It betta fi lose yuh time dan yuh character

It is better to lose your time than to lose your character

Protect your integrity at all costs.

89. Laffi laffi easy fi lie dung

He who laughs a lot is easy to lie down

Take life seriously or you may be used or abused by others who will make wrong assumptions about your character.

90. Man noh hab goudy im satisfy wid bottle

A man who doesn't have a calabash is satisfied with a bottle

Be grateful for the little that you have, though you may yearn for more.

91. Man weh shit a pass noh memba, ah di one weh clean ih

The man who defecates on the road doesn't remember it but the person who cleans it does

The person who has done wrong never remembers, but the one who has been wronged never forgets it.

92. Mannas tek yuh thru di worl

(Good) manners will take you throughout the world

There are benefits to be derived from having good manners.

93. Me noh call yuh noh come

If I don't call you please don't come

Don't go where you are not welcome.

94. Mi throw mi corn mi noh call no fowl

I throw my corn I called no fowls

A guilty conscience will feel the target of a general comment even if it was never intended for them.

95. Monkey deh hide but im tail heng ah doah

A monkey is hiding but his tail is exposed

Some people do all they can to conceal their activities or possessions not realising that others are fully aware of them.

96. Monkey play di figgle mek baboon dance

Monkeys play the fiddle while baboons dance

Some people just wait for someone to take the lead before they start to make a fool of themselves. (One fool makes many)

97. Nebber squeeze ah dawg tail fi si if im ah sleep

Never squeeze a dog's tail to ascertain whether it is asleep

Avoid stirring up trouble by upsetting peaceful people.

98. New broom sweep clean but ole broom know corner

A new broom sweeps clean but an old broom is familiar with the corners

Don't ignore your old friends when new ones appear.

99. Noh count ten toe in front ah man wid nine toe

Don't count your ten toes in the presence of aman who has nine toes

Be sensitive to other people's weaknesses; act with discretion.

100. Noh drive fly fram anodda man cow kin

Don't drive away flies from another man's cow skin

Mind your own business and leave other people's alone.

101. Noh eat food when ih hat

Don't eat your food when it's hot

Allow situations to settle before attempting to address them; never do so when tempers are flaring.

102. Noh fling stoane behine yuh

Do not throw stones behind you

Be aware of, and always remember your roots.

103. Noh mek nobady know yuh last wod

Don't allow anyone to know your last word

Don't let people know your thoughts and plans and don't disclose everything you know.

104. Noh mek one donkey choke yuh

Don't allow a donkey to choke you

Don't allow yourself to be misled by a fool.

105. Noh mek yuh sail too big fi yuh ship

Do not make your sail too big for your ship

Don't engage in activities merely to show off when in effect you are unable to sustain them; be aware of your limitations.

106. "Noh mine" mek ship run ashore

"Don't mind" causes ships to run aground

i) Avoid being passive, get off the fence and have a point of view!
ii) A careless/indifferent attitude doesn't help any situation.

107. Noh care how boar hog try fi hide under sheep wool im grunt always betray im

No matter how a boar pig tries to hide under sheep wool his grunt always betrays him

No matter how much a person tries to disguise himself, the true character will eventually shine through.

108. Noh put yuself inna barrel when match box can hole yuh

Don't put yourself into a barrel when a match box can hold you

Don't pretend to be more accomplished than you are.

109. Noh fatten cackroach fi fowl

Don't fatten cockroaches for fowls

Beware of ungrateful people; don't allow people to exploit you.

110. Noh trubble trubble till trubble tek yuh

Don't interfere with trouble until trouble finds you

Steer clear of trouble but defend yourself if necessary.

111. One han wash di other

One hand washes the other

Try to help others while you can, there will come a time when you too will need assistance.

112. One yeye man ah king inna bline man country

A one-eyed man is a king in a blind man's country

People will hold you in high esteem if they feel that you are better than them in some way.

113. Patience an sweet talk mek monkey mate wid puss

Patience and sweet talk lets a monkey mate with a cat

Diplomacy allows you to open doors; be tactful!

114. Patient man ride danki

A patient man rides the donkey

With patience you can overcome even the most stubborn challenge.

115. Peacock hide im foot wen im ear bout im tail

A peacock hides its foot when it hears about its tail

Proud people take extreme measures in order to hide their weaknesses.

116. Platn waan ded ih go ah hillside go shoot

If a plantain tree wants to die it goes to a hillside to bear

If you insist on courting danger it will find you.

117. Play wid big dawg big dawg bite yuh

If you play with a big dog it will bite you

Associating with people of higher social standing or who have significantly more resources can be painful for those who cannot compete.

118. Play wid puppy, puppy lick yuh mouth

If you play with a puppy it will lick your mouth

If you socialise with ignorant people, they will eventually disrespect you. (Familiarity breeds contempt)

119. Rain doan fall fram di bottom up

The rain doesn't fall from the bottom upwards

i) Those at the top must start and those below will follow;
ii) People at the top must set example for those below.

120. Rotten wood cyaan mek furniture

Rotten wood cannot be used to make furniture

Something bad cannot produce something that is good.

121. Same knife stick sheep stick goat

The same knife that sticks a sheep will stick a goat

Whatever someone does to another he can also do to you; beware of such people!

122. Scratch ole ooman bak an shi wi mek yuh tase ar peppapot

Scratch the back of an old woman and she'll allow you to taste her pepper-pot

Be kind and you will receive kindness. (One good deed deserves another)

123. See an bline hear an deaf

See and blind hear and deaf

Mind your own business.

124. Sick no kya docta wosser

If the sick doesn't care, the doctor won't care either

If you don't care about your problems, Other people won't care either

125. Silent rivva run deep

A silent river runs deep

"Quiet" people are not necessarily quiet; there is often a lot more to them than meets the eye.

126. Si mi an com lib wid mi ah two different ting

To see me and to come and live with me are two different things

You never truly know someone until you have actually had close interaction or actually share a residence with them.

127. Some people know yuh wen ah moon-shine but ah dark nite dem shake dem fiah-tick inna yuh feace

Some people acknowledge you on moonshine nights but when the night is dark they shake their fire-sticks in your face

People want to associate with you are prospering but pretend they don't know you during the hard times.

128. Sorry fi mawga dawg, mawga dog tun roun bite yuh

You have pity on a meagre dog but he in turn bites you

People can be ungrateful.

129. Speak wen spoken to, ansa wen called

Speak when you are spoken to, answer when you are called

Do not interfere into other people's business if it does not concern you.

130. Spida an fly cyaan mek bargin

Spiders and flies cannot make bargains

It is difficult to be friends with someone whom you cannot trust.

131. Strong man bill pass mek weak man walk

A strong man clears the path for a weaker man to use

Those who are strong have a duty to help those who are weak.

132. Sweep yuh own doah befoe yuh see fi mi

Sweep your own doorway before noticing mine

Sort out your own life before criticising or attacking other people.

133. Sweet wood blaze but im noh keep fire

A sweet wood blazes but doesn't keep fire

A man of good character may express his anger, but he bears no grudge thereafter.

134. Talk an tase yuh tongue

Talk and taste your tongue

Think before you speak.

135. Tan an see noh pwoil noh dance

Stay and look doesn't cause any trouble

Look but don't touch.

136. Tan fur si betta

Stay far and get a better view

It is often better to observe some situations from a distance rather than actually getting involved in it.

137. Tief noh love fi si tief carry lang bag

A thief doesn't like to see another thief carry a long bag

A dishonest person doesn't like to see his peers flourishing.

138. To much ah one ting good fi nutting

Too much of the same thing is good for nothing

Avoid excessive behaviour, strive for moderation instead.

139. Trubble deh a bush Anancy bring ih come ah yaad

There's trouble in the Bush, Anancy bringsit home

Be careful not to invite trouble into your life by trying too hard to help someone.

140. Trubble mek de man money mek di manstah

Trouble makes the man, money makes the monster

Challenges build people's character but the love of money destroys it.

141. Two jackass cyaan bray ah di same time

Two jackasses cannot bray at the same time

People must not speak all at once; it is important to listen to each other.

142. Want all lose all

If you want all you'll lose all

Those who want everything for themselves
may end up getting nothing.

143. Wanti wanti caan get ih, getti getti noh want ih

Those who want it cannot get it, those who get/have it don't want it

Those who want something badly often
cannot get it while those who have it
don't appreciate it.

144. Wah good fi di goose good fi di gander

What is good for the goose is good for the gander

Treat people fairly!

145. Wat dawg si im bark all night ram goat si ih noh trouble im

What a dog sees makes it bark all night; a ram goat sees it but it doesn't trouble him

People are affected differently and behave accordingly in situations.

146. Weh dawgs are not invited bones are not provided

Where dogs are not invited bones are not provided

Don't go where you are not welcome.

147. Wen ashes cole dawg sleep in dey

When ashes are cold a dog will sleep in it

When people lose their power, others take liberties/advantage.

148. Wen belly full man bruk pot

When a man's belly is full he breaks the pot

Once people get what they want their interest wanes.

149. Wen bull foot bruk im nyam wid monkey

When a bull's foot is broken he eats with monkeys

When the mighty falls he makes friends with the humble.

150. Wen coco ripe ih muss buss

When a cocoa is ripe it must burst out of its pod

Whatever is on your mind will be revealed in due course.

151. Wen cotton tree come down nanny goat jump over ih

When a cotton tree falls, a nanny goat jumps over it

When the mighty falls the weak triumphs.

152. Wen dawg lib well im trubble cow, cow kick im

When a dog has a good life he interferes with cows and they kick him

People who have nothing to do will interfere with others and eventually get hurt.

153. Wen herring mawga im bone show

When a herring is meagre, its bones protrude

Evil deeds will eventually be exposed.

154. Wen Jackass back strong dem overload im hamper

When a donkey is strong its owner tends to overload its hamper

Good workers are usually given more than their fair share of work to do.

155. Wen Jackass smell caarn im gellop

When a horse smells corn it gallops

If you treat people well they will work hard. ("Encouragement sweetens labour)

156. Wen jankro fly too high im fedda fall

When a crow flies too high it loses its feathers

If you act like you are better than everyone else you will eventually be humbled.

157. Wen pot full ih ovaflow

When a pot is full it overflows

If you continuously provoke people
one day they will retaliate.

158. Wen rat like fi romp roun puss jaw one day im gwine en up inna puss craw

When a rat likes to romp around a cat's jaw, one day it will end up in the cat's craw

If you flirt with danger, you will eventually get hurt.

159. Wen yuh go ah fireside an si food eat half an lef half

When you go to a fireside and see some food, eat half of it and leave the other half

Don't disclose everything you know; keep some information to yourself.

160. Wen yuh go ah Jackass yaad yuh noh fi chat bout big aise

When you go to a Jackass' yard, do not talk About big ears

Avoid saying anything that could be construed as a criticism or insult to someone while you are on their property.

161. Wen yuh han inna lian mouth tek time draw ih out

When your hand is in a lion's mouth, carefully draw it out

When you are in a vulnerable position you must be humble.

162. Wen yuh neighbour beard ketch ah fiah tek wahta wet fi yuh

If you see your neighbour's beard on fire, use water to wet yours

Learn from other people's experiences; don't wait until it happens to you!

163. Wen yuh see others ah jump pon two leg yuh jump pon one

When you see others jumping on two legs, you must jump on one only

Don't follow the crowd; there is nothing wrong with being different.

164. Weh yuh boun yuh mus obey

Where you are bound you must obey

Honour your commitments and fulfil your responsibilities.

165. Who di cap fit mek dem wear it

Whoever the cap fits should be allowed to wear it

A guilty conscience will always feel targeted.

166. Words inna mout ah noh load pan head

Words of the mouth are not loads on the head

Don't allow people's words to hurt you, ignore them!

167. Yeye fi si an aise fi hear but mout mus shut

The eyes should see and ears should hear but the mouth must remain closed

Listen and observe but don't participate in gossip.

168. Yuh get yuh han inna deble mout tek time tek ih out

If you put your hand in the devils mouth, take it out carefully

Exercise caution when you find yourself in tricky situations.

169. Yuh can hide an buy lan but yuh cyaan hide an wuk ih

You can hide and buy land but you can't hide and work on it

What is in the dark will ultimately be revealed.

170. Yuh come yah fi drink milk yuh noh come yah fi count cow!

You came here to drink milk, not to count cows

Accept people's kindness and don't meddle in their business; keep your business relationships professional.

171. Yuh cyaan expect anyting from a hog but a grunt

You can't expect anything from a pig but a grunt

People are true to their character, even if they try to hide it.

172. Yuh cyaan mek a silk purse outta pig aise

You cannot use a pig's ear to make a silk purse

You cannot change people.

173. Yuh cyaan siddong pon cow back an cuss cow kin

You cannot sit on a cow's back and curse the cow's skin

If you are dependent on someone you should not be disrespectful to them.

174. Yuh cyaan tap bud from fly ova yuh head but yuh can tap im fram mek nes in deh

You cannot prevent a bird from flying over your head but you can stop him from making a nest in it

You will meet and have dealings with people of questionable character but it is you who ultimately determines who becomes your friend.

175. Yuh cyaan tek medicine fi smaddy else

You cannot take medicine for someone else

Everyone must expect to shoulder his own responsibility.

176. Yuh cyaan cut off yuh nose fi spite yuh feace

You must not cut off your nose in order to spite your face

Don't take actions that will ultimately hurt you just to get even with someone.

177. Yuh fallaw fool yuh fool yuself

If you follow a fool, you become a fool yourself

Be mindful of the company you keep.

178. Yuh noh done breed so noh laugh afta yuh granny

If you are still of child-bearing age, don't laugh at your grandmother

Be respectful to the elderly; one day you too will be old.

179. Yuh promise sensé fowl anyting im ah look fi ih

If you make a promise to a chicken, he expects you to keep it

Don't make promises you cannot keep.

180. Yuh pushi, pushi, pushi till yuh shub ih

You push it, push it and push it until you shove it

If you consistently pester someone they will eventually retaliate.

Part II

Things Jamaican

Food and Drink

Barbecue chicken

Escoveitch Fish

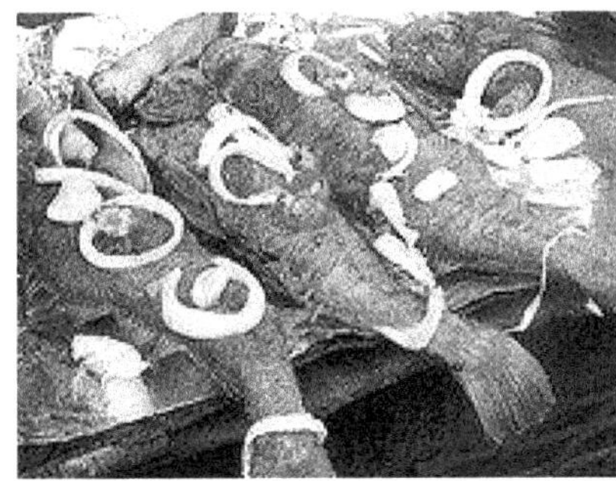

Jerk Chicken

Ackee and Saltfish
a breakfast favourite

Bammy
Often served with fish

Rice and peas
& chicken
Favourite Sunday dinner

Rum

Jamaica produces the widest variety of rum in the world (white, dark, spiced, aged, overproof, golden & vintage). Jamaican rum is the key ingredient in Jamaican rum punch, another Jamaican favourite.

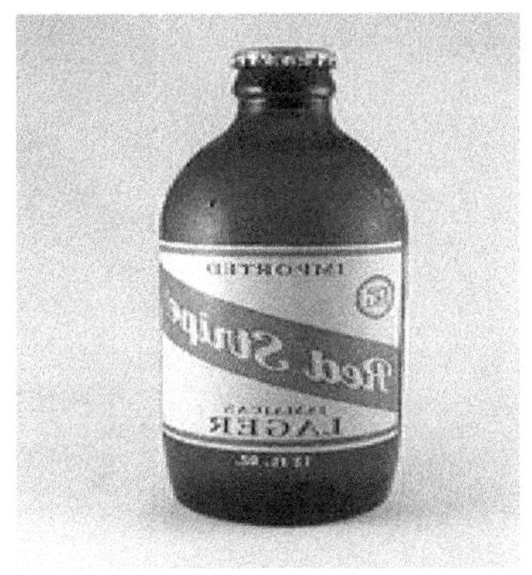

Red Stripe Beer

A favourite in Jamaica and famous around the world for its great taste and refreshing qualities.

Ginger Beer

Made with real Jamaican root ginger, this refreshing fiery drink is often served over ice with a sprig of mint and a wedge of lime. Also used as a mixer.

Coffee

There are two main types of Jamaican coffee - Jamaica Blue Mountain and Jamaica Prime. Blue Mountain must be grown in prescribed areas of the Blue Mountains. Jamaica Prime is grown in other areas.

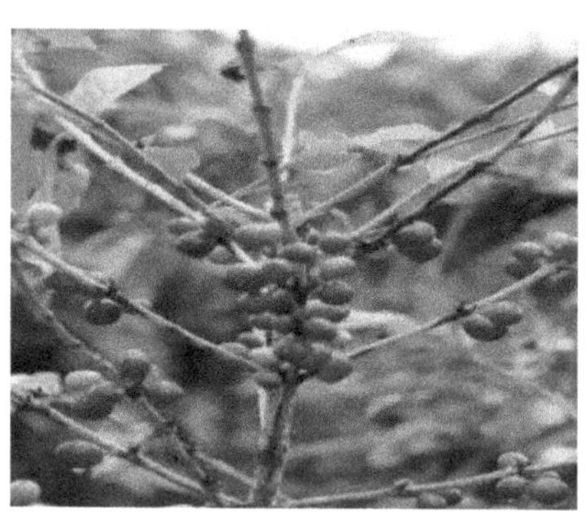

Sorrel (Roselle)

High in vitamin C Jamaican Sorrel is a rich and tasty drink, consumed particularly at Christmas- time. Jamaican sorrel aids in reducing inflammation.

Irish moss

This seaweed grows on rocks in Jamaica. It makes a refreshing drink and is considered an excellent remedy for a number of conditions. Jamaican Irish moss is believed to boost sexual prowess.

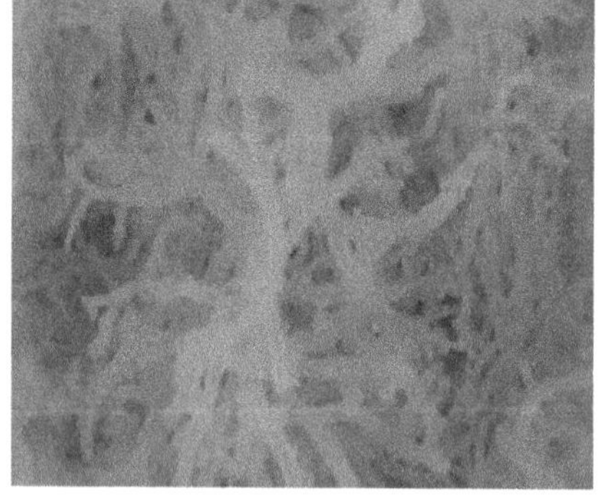

Flora

Banana
Jamaica [produces bananas for export and local use. Bananas are a very popular Jamaican food that is used in many Jamaican recipes. The fruit is eaten ripe or green.

Ackee
The ackee is Jamaica's national fruit and the main ingredient in Jamaica's national dish

Coconut
Jamaican coconut is used in many recipes such as rice and peas, grater cake, coconut drops and many others. Green coconut produces a jelly and very refreshing drink.

Soursop (Graviola)

The Jamaican soursop has several vitamins, minerals, protein, carbohydrates, fiber, ash, calcium, phosphorus, iron, vitamin A, thiamine, riboflavin, niacin, ascorbic acid and amino acids.

Aloe Vera (Sinkle Bible)

Aloe Vera is a popular plant which contains various medicinal and cleansing properties.

Pimento

The dried, unripe berries from the pimento tree are used extensively in Jamaican cooking and give food a distinctive Jamaican flavour. Pimento berries are an important ingredient for Jamaican favourite dishes.

Jamaican Tea

Cerasee
(Momordica Charantia)
A bitter tasting tea believed to cleanse the blood and help in the prevention of colds, flu, headaches, jaundice and stomach ache. It is also said to reduce the risk of lung cancer, heart disease, and high blood pressure.

Fever Grass
Otherwise called lemon grass, fever grass has a soothing, light lemon flavour. It is believed to provide relief from nervous headaches, stomach and urinary problems, and help to speed up recovery from fever.

Dandelion
This is used for as a diuretic and laxative. It is also used as a remedy for rheumatism, haemorrhoids, gout, eczema, other skin conditions, and diabetes. It is said to promote the flow of bile and stimulate the appetite.

Peppermint

Peppermint and black mint teas are popular breakfast beverages, but can be consumed at any time of the day. Peppermint is said to provide relief from nausea, headache and vomiting.

Cola Nut (Bissy)

Bissy is regarded for its medicinal properties because of its effect as an antidote for poisons. It is said to relieve menstrual cramps, headache, gout, rheumatism, jaundice, vomiting, nausea and indigestion. It is also used to control diabetes and obesity.

Leaf of life (Bryophyllum Pinnatum)

This is used to treat hypertension, colds, bruises, boils, ulcers, insect bites, earaches, sprains, swelling, colds, arthritis, asthma, high blood pressure, swellings, sprains, boils and abscesses.

Flowers

Bouganvillea

Orchid

Hibiscus

Anthurium

Ginger Lily

Crotons

Fauna

Woodpecker

Jamaica's bird population contains about 280 species of which 30 are endemic

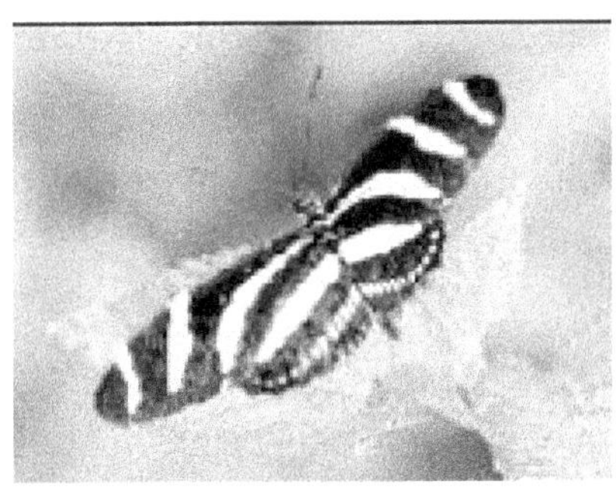

Zebra Butterfly

Jamaica has some 134 butterfly and moth species of which 20 are endemic.

Jamaican Coney

Terrestrial land mammal found in the rocky, forested areas of Jamaica.

Jamaican Iguana

One of the largest native land animals (endangered)

Saltwater Crocodile

Crocodiles are protected under the Wild Life Protection Act; it is illegal to catch, or kill them. It is also an offence to have a crocodile or any part of the animal in one's possession.

Green Anole

One of the 7 species of Anolis present on the island.

Medicinal Herbs Grown in Jamaica

Arrow Root
Aloe Vera/Sinkle-Bible (*Aloe barbadensis)*
Bissy
Bitterwood
Blood wisp
Cayenne pepper
Cerasse
Chainy Root/Wild yam root/China Root (*Smilax balbisiana)*
Cinnamon
Comfrey (*Symphytum officinale)*
CornSilk -The hair of the corn
Dandelion/Wild coffee (*Taraxacum officinale)*
Dog blood
Dogwood *(Piscidia erythrina/Piscidia piscipula)*
Duppy gun
Fresh Cut
Fever Grass *(Andropogon citrates/ Cymbopogon citrates)*
Garlic
Ginger
Ginkgo/Ginkgo biloba
Hog Head
Marijuana/Ganja
Jack in a bush (*Eupatorium odoratum)*
John Charles
Leaf of life (*Bryophyllum pinnatum)*
Medina
Nettle/Stinging Nettle *(Urtica urens/Urtica dioica)*
Orange peel
Periwinkle/Ramgoat roses
Quassia chips
Red Clover
Samson/bee bush
Sarsaparilla *(Smilax ornate)*
Shame-a-Macca/Shane O Lady
Siberian ginseng
Sorrel
Soursop (*Annona muricata)*
Spanish Needle
Spirit Weed
Stiff cock
Strong back
Vervine/love bush
Yohimbe

Dignitaries & famous people who visited Jamaica post Independence

1962 - Her Royal Highness Princess Margaret
1962 - Lyndon Johnson, Vice President, United States
1965 - Dr. Martin Luther King, Civil Rights Leader, USA National Hero
1966 - Mohammed Ali
1966, 1986 Mother Teresa
1966, 1983, 2002 Her Majesty Queen Elizabeth II and HRH Prince Philip
1966 - HRH Prince Charles and Princess Anne
1966 - His Imperial Majesty Haile Selassie I, Emperor of Ethiopia
1966 - President Kenneth Kaunda of Zambia
1971 - Edson Arantes Do Nascimento (Pele)
1971 - President Jose Figueres, Costa Rica
1973 - George Foreman and Joe Frazier (World Heavyweight Title Fight)
1974 - President Julius Nyerere of Tanzania
1975 - President Samora Moises Machel, Mozambique
1977, 2000, 2005 President Fidel Castro, Cuba
1982 - President Ronald Reagan, United States of America
1982 - President Karl Carstens, Germany
1982 - President Louis Herrerra Campin, Venezuela
1986 - Archbishop Desmond Tutu, South Africa
1987 - Rt. Hon. Margaret Thatcher, Prime Minister of Britain
1987 - President Miguel de la Madrid, Mexico

1987 - President Dr. Auelt Masire, Botswana

1991 - Mr. Nelson Mandela, Leader of the ANC, South Africa

1993 - Pope John Paul II

1994 - General Colin Powell, First African American Secretary of State, USA

1995 - President Robert Mugabe, Zimbabwe

1997 - President Jerry Rawlings, Ghana

1998 - Kofi Annan, United Nations Secretary General

2000 - HRH Prince Phillip, England

2002 - President Olusegun Obasanjo, Nigeria

2002, 2011 Louis Farrakhan, Leader of the Nation of Islam

2004 - President Thabo Mbeki, South Africa

2007 - President Luiz Inacio Lula da Silva, Brazil

2007 - Dr. John Sentamu, Archbishop of York

2009 - King Juan Carlos I and Queen Sophia

2009 - President Jakaya Mrisho Kikwete, United Republic of Tanzania

2010 - Hilary Clinton, Secretary of State, USA

2012 - Prince Harry of Wales (UK)

Jamaican Parishes

Where to go and what to do

Clarendon

- Have an invigorating soak at the curative waters of Milk River Bath
- Visit Portland Point Lighthouse
- Visit St Peter’s Church and Moneymusk Library
- Visit Jamaica's annual Agricultural Society's Farm Show at Denbigh
- Visit Colbeck Castle Great House

Hanover

- Visit Tryall Estate
- Go hiking behind the hills of cousins cove
- Visit Maryland Falls
- Visit The Great Morass crocodile habit
- Visit Bloody Bay

Kingston & St Andrew

- Climb the Blue Mountains
- Visit Devon House for gifts and ice cream
- Visit a theatre
- Tour the national Gallery
- Enjoy Carnival after Easter
- Dine and party in New Kingston
- Visit Hope Gardens
- Visit the Craft Market
- Visit The St Andrew Parish Church, built in 1700

- View the Half-Way-Tree Clock and tower built in 1913 as a memorial to King Edward VII of England
- Go snorkelling at Lime Cay (featured in the film “The Harder they Come”)
- Visit Port Royal
- Visit the Bob Marley Museum
- Visit Rockfort Mineral Bath

Manchester

- Go hiking and horseback riding
- Take an eco tour
- Go birdwatching at Marshall's Pen Great House
- Visit Little Ochie
- Tour he High Mountain Coffee and Chocolate Factory at Williamsfield, the Pickapepper Sauce Factory at Shooters Hill and the Bammy Factory in Mandeville
- Visit the gallery at Bloomfield Great House,

Portland

- Visit the Morant Point Lighthouse
- Experience the mysterious waters of Blue Lagoon
- Go Hiking
- Visit Boston Beach, Long bay Beach, Winifred’s Beach, San San Beach and Frenchman’s Cove
- Have a taste of Jamaica at Boston Jerk
- Visit Pelew Island
- Visit Navy Island (formerly owned by Errol Flyn)
- Visit Crystal springs
- Go Surfing and Sport Fishing
- Visit Reach Falls
- Go Rafting on the Rio Grande
- Visit Nanny Town

St Ann

- Visit Dolphin Cove
- Purchase souvenirs at the Craft Markets
- Climb Dunn's River Falls
- Go snorkelling, windsurfing and diving
- Visit Nine Mile, the birthplace and shrine of Robert (Bob) Nesta Marley
- View the historical architecture of Harmony Hall
- Visit Wassi Art and see the creation of extraordinary handmade pottery
- Go horseback riding
- Visit the New Hope Great House and the ruins of the Minard Great House.
- Experience Fern Gully – 3 Miles of foliage lined with hundreds of species of fern said to be the largest fern arboretum in the world
- Visit the "Noisy Water" River Cave and "Rat Bat Hole".
- Sample the hearty treats of Faiths Pen
- Visit Green Grotto Caves
- Visit Ocho Rios Marine Park, Shaw
- Park Gardens and the Coyaba River Garden
- Visit Seville Heritage Park and Columbus Park Museum
- Experience Chukka Cove Adventures
- Go White River Rafting
- Swim with dolphins at Dolphin Cove
- **Go glass-bottom kayaking** on the Caribbean Sea
- Visit the Walker's Wood Farm and Craft Market
- Take the Jamaica Bobsled ride
- Enjoy a Mystic Mountain escapade
- See Marcus Garvey Statue in St. Ann's Bay

- Visit the ruins of Edinburgh Castle
- Visit the Watt Town Zion Church spiritual schoolroom
- Go River Tubing at White River Valley Adventure

St. Catherine

- See the Bog Walk Gorge
- Visit the Rio Cobre
- Enjoy fish and festival at Hellshire beach
- Visit Linstead Market and the Linstead Anglican Church
- Visit Caymanas Park & Golf & Country Club
- Visit Guardsman Serenity Park
- Visit Rodney Memorial and St. Jago de la Vega Cathedral, Spanish Town
- Visit Portmore – Jamaica's third city
- Visit the People's Museum of Craft & Technology & White Marl Taino Museum

St. Elizabeth (South Coast)

- Take a boat ride up the Black River
- Visit Treasure Beach
- Experience Tiers of cascading water at YS Falls
- Take a tour through the headquarters of Appleton rum
- Go Bird Watching
- Visit Alligator Pond and alligator hole
- Take in the view of Pedro Bluff, Cutlass Bay and Lovers Leap
- Enjoy a taste of mouth-watering seafood at Little Ochie
- Drive through Bamboo Ave - nature's perfect archway

St. James

- Visit Rose Hall Great House
- Play Golf
- Explore the hidden caves, trails and waterfalls in the Cockpit Country
- Wine and dine at the Hip Strip
- Enyoy Reggae Sumfest in summer
- Go Rafting on the Martha Brae
- Visit the sun-splashed
- shores of Doctors Cave Beach
- Go cliff diving
- Have a great night out and listen to Live Music
- Rent a bike

St. Mary

- Visit Goldeneye where Ian Flemming created James Bond
- Tour Firefly museum - former home of Noel Coward artist, actor and playwright
- Visit the Rio Nuevo, White River and the Wag Water river
- Visit Castleton Botanical Gardens

St. Thomas

- Visit the springs at Bath; visit bull bay and Cane River Falls
- Visit Zion Hill, a site populated by Bobo shanty rastafarians
- Visit the Queensbury Ridge monument to Three-Finger" Jack Mansong, an "eighteenth century "Robin Hood" character

Trelawny

- Visit an underground spring and watch mystical waters illuminate a tropical night.
- Visit the Rock Spring Caves and the Quashie River Sink Caves
- Visit Stewart Castle in Duncans
- Visit the Baptist Manse on Market Street near the waterfront
- Visit the Reggae to Wear garment factory

Westmoreland

- Visit the mausoleum at Grange Hill
- Visit the Roaring River and Cave
- Visit Bluefields Beach and Kool Runnings Water Park
- See the Peter Tosh Memorial

GLOSSARY

Afi – has/have to
Agaen – again
Ah – at/it is
Ah fi – it belongs to
Ah good – serves you right
Ahoa - Oh
Aise – ears
Alms ouse – nonsense
Anansi – spider
Anodda – another
Ar – her
Av – have
Ax – ask
Baaskit – basket
Backa – behind
Backle – bottle
Bad mout –speak ill of
Bad mine – jealous/ grudgeful
Bakansa – sharp answer
Bafan – clumsy/awkward
Bandoolu – dishonest
Bangarang – disturbance/noise
Bankra – big basket
Barn – born
Bat – moth
Battam – bottom
Beanie – small
Befoe – before
Ben de – was/were
Berry – very
Bex – upset/angry
Bickle – food
Bickle – food
Big and so-so-so – big-bodied & lazy
Bline – blind
Brawta – extra
Breda – brother
Breshé – breadfruit
Bruk – break/broke
Bud – bird
Bun – burn
Bun – burn
Buss - burst
Bwile – boil
Bwoy – boy
Cackroach – cockroach
Carry-go bring-come – gossip
Cawna – corner
Chowziz – pants
Chuck – truck
Chupid – stupid
Cliding – cloying
Cobich – mean/stingy

Coco – cocoa
Com yah – come here
Coodeh – look at that
Craben – craven
Crakup - laugh
Cratch – scratch
Crawny – look
Awful/unwell
Crawses – problematic situation/person
Cruff – untidy/ unambitious
Cry-cry – cries easily
Cumbulo – peers
Cumfat - comfort
Cunnyman – conman
Cunue – canoe
Cuss – to quarrel
Cuss-cuss – quarrel
Cut yeye – to look at someone in isdain
Cuya – look at this
Cyaan – cannot
Dan – than
Danki – donkey
Dat – that
Dawg – dog
De - the
Deble – devil
Ded lef – inheritance
Dégé dégé – only
Deh – there/is
Deh deh – is there
De bout – around/nearby
Dem – them
Di – the
Diay – day
Doah – door
Doan – don't
Dongkia – carefree
Doze – those
Dress back – step back/ reverse
Dung – down
Duont it? – isn't that so?
Duppy – ghost
Dut – earth/soil
Dutty – dirty
Dweet – do it
Ebery – every
Ef - if
Ef a so, a so – so be it
Facety – feisty/saucy
Fah – for
Fall dung – fall
Fallaw – follow
Fala bak a mi – follow me
Fambily – family
Farrid – forehead
Fass – inquisitive
Fasser - faster
Fedda – feather
Fenké fenké – slight/weak

Fi – for/to
Fiah – fire
Firetick – fire-stick
Fiwi – ours
Flim – film
Fluxy – flaccid/squashy
Fool-fool – silly/stupid
Foot bottam – sole of the foot
Force ripe – unnaturally mature
Frak tail – hemline
Frouzi – smelly
Fur – far
Gaah farin – go abroad
Gahlang – go on
Gastu – must
Get chruu – succeed
Ghana – gone to
Ginal – trickster/ dishonest person
Gi a six fi a nain – deceive
Goh – go
Goh dung – go down
Gonna – going to...
Gravalicious – greedy
Grung – ground/ cultivated field
Guweh – go away
Gwaan – go on
Gwine – going to
Gyal – girl
Haad – hard
Hab – has/have
Hackle – hassle/bother
Haffi – have/has to
Halla – holler/cry out loudly
Han – hand
Han middle – palm
Hat - painful
Hea - hear
Head top – crown of the head
Hebby – heavy
Heng – hang
Henka – hanging around for food
Hitey titey – snobbish
Hush – be comforted
Ih-he – yes
Ih – It
Ih-ih – no
Im – him
Inna – in /into
Jankro – vulture/crow
Jankro Batty – Unpurified white rum
Jing-bang – lots of useless items
Jook – pierce/poke
Jrap fut – to dance
Juck - pierce

Junjo – mould
Kak op – to raise
Keba – cover
Kekkle – kettle/ pot
Ketch – catch/caught
Kibba - cover
Kin pupalick – to do a somersault
Kin teet – grin
Kot ten – to sit with legs crossed
Krai kree – to call time-out
Krismus – Christmas
Kuh ya – look here
Kumoochin – mean/stingy
Kuul-yu-fut – relax
Kya – care
Labba labba – gossip
Laffi-laffi – giggly
Laka se - as if
Lang – long
Langa – longer
Larn – learn
Lenky – lanky
Lib – live
Libati tekin – presumptious attitude
Libba – liver
Lick - hit
Licky licky – suck up to/ greedy
Likkle – little
Lilly – little
imba – limber
Lob – love
Lyad – liar
Ma – mother/madam
Macca – thorn
Mada – mother
Maggige – maggot
Mannas – manners
Mash up – destroy/ break up
Maskitta – mosquito
Massa – mister
Mawga – meagre /malnourished
Meja - measure
Mek – make
Memba – remember
Mi – me
Miehke-miehke – messy/distasteful
Mikhase – hurry up
Mout – mouth
Mout-a-massy – someone who talks too much
Mucky – filthy
Mumma – mother
Munstah – monster
Mussi – must
Muss-muss – mouse

Naah – not going to
Nebber – never
Nize – noise
Noh – does not
Nowey - nowhere
Nuff – plenty/brazen
Nutten – nothing
Nutting – nothing
Nyam – eat
Oddah – other
Ooman – woman
Outa haada – rude/ imprudent
Out fi – about to
Owna – owner
Packi - vessel made from a gourd
Pan – on
Passa passa – mix up
Patoo – owl
PawPaw – papaya
Peenywally – firefly
Peteta – potato
Pickney – young child
Picky-picky – choosey/ sparse
Poah – poor
Poppyshow – laughable/ show off
Pread – spread
Prekeh – one who thinks much of himself but is in fact a laughing stock
Pupa – father
Pushi – push it
Puss – cat
Putto-putto – soft
Puttus – sweetheart
Pwoil – spoil
Pyaa-pyaa – sickly/feeble
Quint – blink
Ramp – play
Red yeye – envious
Renk – foul smell/rude
Rivva – river
Roun – around
Run a boat – informal cooking
Sa – sir
Sabe – save
Saggle – saddle
Sake a – because of
Seame weigh – just like that
Sarry – sorry
Seh feh – dare me
Shaat – short
Shaata – shorter
Shedda – shadow
Sheg up – to disappoint
Shi – she
Shuub – shove/push
Si – see
Siddong – sit down

Sinting – something
Slackniss – lewd/
vulgar behaviour
Sleep up – coagulate
Smaddy – somebody
Soppm – something
Sopsy – weak/soft/puny
Spirit tek – have an
affinity with
Stranja – stranger
Stush – snobbish
Se-se – gossip
Su-su – to gossip
Swallaw – swallow
Stush – snobbish
Su-su – carry news/gossip
Swo-so – mediocre
Tallawah – impressive
Tan – stand/stay/is
Tan deh – stay there
Tan up – stand up
Tap – Stop/top
Tea – any hot drink
Teddy – steady
Tegereg – person of
no class/uncouth
Tek – take
Tenk yuh – thank you
Tick – stick
Ticker – thicker
Ticky ticky – young
children/fish
Tideh – today
Ting – thing
Togeda – together
Trampooz – to walk about
Trow – throw
Trubble – trouble
Tun – turn
Uhnu – you all
Umhm – yes
Waagen? – what else?
Waah - want
Wah – what
Wallah – wallow
Warra warra – (used
instead of a curseword)
Wash – sugar & water
mixed
Weh – where/away
Wha – what
Wha-ah gwaan – what's
happening?
Wha mek –why
Whappen – what's up?
Wi – we
Wid – with
Wingy – small/feeble
Wod – word
Woss – worse/worst
Wosser – worse
Wuk – work
Wukliss – worthless
Yah – here

Yasso – here
Yeye – eye

Yout – youth
Yuh – you

www.ingramcontent.com/pod-product-compliance
Ingram Content Group UK Ltd.
Pitfield, Milton Keynes, MK11 3LW, UK
UKHW020239250726
13967UKWH00001B/451

9 781471 688874